rosanna deerchild

calling down the sky

BookLand
press

Published by BookLand Press
15 Allstate Parkway, Suite 600
Markham, Ontario L3R 5B4
www.booklandpress.com

Printed and bound in Canada

Front cover image by Mary Scott

Library and Archives Canada Cataloguing in Publication

Deerchild, Rosanna, author
    Calling down the sky / Rosanna Deerchild.

(Canadian Aboriginal voices)
Poems.
Issued in print and electronic formats.
ISBN 978-1-77231-005-4 (pbk.).--ISBN 978-1-77231-006-1 (epub).--
ISBN 978-1-77231-007-8 (pdf)

    I. Title. II. Series: Canadian Aboriginal voices

PS8607.E445C34 2015   C811'.6   C2015-902506-0
                                           C2015-902507-9

Canada Council Conseil des arts
for the Arts   du Canada

ONTARIO ARTS COUNCIL
CONSEIL DES ARTS DE L'ONTARIO
an Ontario government agency
un organisme du gouvernement de l'Ontario

We acknowledge the support of the Canada Council for the Arts, which last year invested $157 million to bring the arts to Canadians throughout the country. We acknowledge the support of the Ontario Arts Council (OAC), an agency of the Government of Ontario. We acknowledge the financial support of the Ontario Media Development Corporation for our publishing activities.

table of contents

mama's testament: truth and reconciliation

people ask me all the time
about residential schools
as if it's their business or something

ever since that white guy
nete in ottawa said he was sorry

as if
he knows anything about those places

he wasn't there
he doesn't know

he wasn't there
when i needed comfort
when i cried

he doesn't know
what that priest did
what those nuns did

you can't say sorry
for those things
for what happened there

he's got no right

share your story he says
what does that even mean

boy these misti-gu-su
and their fancy talk

share your story
as if it's that easy

anyway
it was a long time ago

fifty years since those days
fifty years i said nothing

the words
they get caught right here
in my throat

where the nuns would grab
when we spoke Cree

as if grabbing a dead duck's neck
haul us up in front of that class

stand there so long
we pissed ourselves

you learn pretty quickly
to stay quiet after that boy

no
we never talk about it

not back home
not with each other
not even when it was happening

you just tried to forget about it
leave it behind

some of us did
some of us are still trying

it always finds you though
drags you back

don't make up stories
that's what they told us kids

when we went back home
told them what was going on
in those schools

still got sent back
every year
less of us came home

still they said nothing
until we were nothing
just empty skins

full of broken english
ruler broken bones
bible broken spirits

and back home
became a broken dream

no damage done
for all but five years

that's what it said in the letter
about my residential school story

dear claimant
no records
no proof

sorry

nine years
that's how long
they kept me in there

i was just a baby
when they came for me

father died on the trapline
mother in the tb sanatorium

didn't even get to say goodbye
never saw them again

nine years
you know what i got for that

deaf in one ear
blind in one eye

scars all over my head
my legs don't work
arthritis

diabetes
from what we ate there
you know i never once saw fruit

can't get no damn sleep
the dead keep me awake eh
ask me for forgiveness

but you can't forgive and forget
the unnameable

there is no word for what they did
in our language

to speak it is to become torn
from the choking

money got no cure for that

now
i'm almost seventy

and you want me to
share my story

ok then
here it is
here in the unwritten
here in the broken lines
of my body that can never forget

two braids

on my first day
of kindergarten

mama weaves
two braids

so tightly
as if they will never let go

too tight i fuss pull
at my temples

she loosens stitches
spit shines them

into long perfect arrows
wraps and wraps

tips into exclamation
points memories

entwined
of her first day at residential school

of falling wisps of hair
of never going home

mama kisses my forehead
lips a warm berry

on my brown skin

sends me on my way
i wave smile back

my braids bounce
behind me

a reminder of who i am
always pointing me

back home

mama loves country

hums
while she cleans

crazy
crazy for feeling

patsy cline
scrubs dishes

dolly's coat of many colours
folded in clothes

please
help me i'm falling

charlie pride
begs mama

as she sweeps
hallway stairs

saves the next tear drop
from freddy fender's

broken heart
to mop floors

georgie jones
strings her along

clothing line sheets
become dance floors

he stopped loving
her today

mama always
forgives him

though

it's hank
she really loves

only senior makes
mama sing

i'm so lonesome
i could cry

says

musta had
hard times

you can hear it
in his voice

i listen hard
to her slow sad songs

and know
just what she means

confession

mama is always just
out of reach

a bird i could watch
but never catch

a closed jar
my small angry hands

could not
open

a language
my clumsy tongue

could not
speak

mama kept herself
a secret

she could not tell
if it was truth or lie

when she slept
i would lean in close

listen
for confession

wonder how she spoke
in dreams

my fingertips
feathers floating

over her mouth
feel only her breath

rising
quick and gone

things i know about my mother as a child

mama bakes me cake
every birthday from scratch

cooks me perfect porridge
tops with milk and brown sugar

or sunny side up eggs
bacon toast crusts cut off

cleans up my mess
washes clothes

mends all my rips and sews dresses
brushes my hair while she hums

mama calls me babe and my girl
but cannot say i love you

a rare gift just for birthdays
lingering hugs only when sick

tells us forgive and forget
but never shows us how

her anger is thrown quick
jagged pieces of glass

swears at us in Cree
we learn to duck the words

falls into silence often her sadness
a dark place she gets lost in

never cries in front of me
but i hear her through doors

mama drinks to forget
something she does not name

broken beer bottles
cigarette butts bruises

thrown at endless parties
rage until crash of sun

stops for a while soon begins
again like a storm rising

mama leaves

a mess
wherever she goes

pieces strewn
throughout her life

everyone always
leaving or taking

papa died
on the trapline

mama
in the tb sanatorium

school broke
the rest

men are nothing
but destruction

even her kids
run from her

mama is storm
falling

falling
hitting the ground

always leaving
bent and broken

limbs heart
spirit

that's all she knows
how to break

a crack in her
bone memory

that is felt
for generations

the first time

long escaped
from small town

i am 25
disconnected

free from the eye
of mama's storm

she calls me
one day full of fear

mama tells me
it's those schools

she says those places
were a hell

they killed us there
they hurt us
so many girls
so many boys

disjointed
pictures

her voice

an urgent rush
of words of tears

her memory a whisper
rising to rage

screams i can't forget
can't forgive

those nuns
are still here

mama's voice
begs me to hear her

to take this story from her
but i am not ready

my angry hands
still cannot hold

our stories together
too thin threads

break between us
mama does not speak

again
the silence blankets

blanket

there's a patch blanket
on the shelf
in the back of my closet

mama made it
when i was a girl
i don't take it out
though don't unravel

squares of sewn together
patches
remnants of things
not quite saved forced
together

mama was careful
in her cutting cautious to sew
rag tag into a design
that made sense

from a distance

but it failed could not
hide protect
make this brown girl
invisible

to those who only see
always uncover
the colour of her skin

mama didn't know
she sewed a disease
in its creases a smallpox
caught from generations before

one patch
for each woman
who died

mama in residential school
her mama from tuberculosis

all the way back
to our first grandmother gifted
that first infected blanket

there's a patch blanket
on the shelf
in the back of my closet

one day i will take it out

loosen a patch free

the second time

i ask mama
about residential school
she says no

i ask her again
she says no

the third time

i stop listen
to her silence

ask about her diabetes
her hip achy back

her sore knees
did she get her hearing aid fixed

whether she thinks it will rain tomorrow
mama talks about all this

says i'm not too good my girl
my sugar is too high

arthritis acting up that damn doctor
won't give me any more pain pills

this hearing aid is shit
and the rain

the rain hurts
my girl

i listen to her talk
back words slow

fill her cup
with tea

over tea

with acknowledgment to rita joe

mama drinks red rose tea
with carnation and splenda

water boiled on stove
in soup pot

three bags steeped
for hours of refills

just like back home
over tea people talk

relatives births
deaths marriages

and bingo
all witnessed

over tea

mama
stirs her cup

slow
measured

tic tic tic
of spoon

over fills
silence

mama lost her talk
in residential school

she sips up memories
the heat burns her tongue

mama's voice

hesitant

like a child
walking barefoot

over sticks
and stones

eyes down
cast

careful
to avoid

mama
who ran reckless

her whole life
who didn't stop

for anyone
not even for her children

mama's voice
stumbles

falls

when i ask
her to recall

that long
untravelled road

to name
those dark places

my question
hurts like a break

in her bone

what is carried

1.

mama ticks off

dates
facts

marks each
with a finger

a checklist
she has kept

folded tucked
away

waiting

2.

mama went to three residential schools

sturgeon landing opened in 1926

> (mama was taken there
> from south indian lake
> in 1950 at five years old)

it burned down in 1952

> (at seven years old)

moved from northern saskatchewan
to northern manitoba

> (no closer to home)

first in the pas

> (near sacred heart
> that mama says still stands
> a middle finger)

then at clearwater lake

> (in 1955)

guy hill residential school

> (mama left in 1959 at 14)

it closed in 1979

3.

mama told those nuns
she'd never forget

knew the day
would come

when those numbers
would be finally exposed

mama
unfolds time

smoothes out
the line

in front of her

on the first day

all us kids had to do it eh

a lot of us cried
huddled together like sheep
bleating and pushing
trying to melt into each other
more scared than we ever been

one by one
peeled off
taken into a little room

us left behind catch
glint of a sharp edge
hear the crying
before door closes

some never had it done
their long perfect braids
a measure of seasons
umbilical cord to mama
earth
a map back home

cut away

just like sheep
go in fat and fluffy
come out bald as babies
except skinny and sick looking

boys buzzed bald
like dandelions
blown of all their wishes

girls bowl cut
into cookie cutter girls

when it's my turn
i climb onto the cold grey chair
look up at the nun
blink terror

she speaks something to me
sounds like an angry crow
holds long scissors like a claw
silver smiles malice at me

crow-nun reaches
i flinch only to be caught
by her other hand

smashes
my head so hard
blood blooms a berry patch
on clean white wall

don't move after that
not for a long time
just sit there
stare big eyed
mute like an owl

watch my hair
fall wisps
of something
i used to be

number 105

grouped
by gender and size

sorted in lines of beds
along dormitory halls

boys on one floor
girls on another

nuns and priests
at both ends

our names erased
given a number

label on desk
stitched on dresses

etched on pine wood
box at foot of bed

my almost coffin
i climb in to hide

when sturgeon landing school
catches fire

my sisters are frantic
search every floor

find me in box number 105
baptized in flame reborn

in smoke my name
my name is ash

sister rose

black bird
half-starved and bald
after a long cold winter
that one

her black habit
a collector of sound
small whimpers
utterance of Cree
catches them all

her small sharp eyes
pins attacking
every untucked shirt
every scuffed shoe

even her voice
sharp and piercing
carves new names
into our hearts

savage
heathen
dirty indian

sister rose
preys on our fear

collects us
like jewels

for the crown of her God

feast

watery oatmeal
like gruel for breakfast

uncooked potato or turnip for lunch
crunch of rawness still makes me sour

bologna macaroni tomato soup at supper
or even cow's blood baked in long pans

cut into squares like jello every day
we never saw fruits or vegetables

until social workers and food inspectors
came a three month countdown to each feast

only time we got to eat
the same as priests or nuns

roast beef gravy creamy mashed potato
even green peas and fresh bread

stuffed my stomach to its brim
hoping to save fullness for later

when at night
i could hear kids crying

then take it out of my pocket and feed them
but always find it empty

bread crumbs

all the time we were hungry
find ways to steal food
us girls we had a plan

after lights out
nuns and kids asleep
sneak out

one at a time
quick soundless
mice across floor

one props door
another steals bread
a third watches out

each night eat
only what we need
just enough to ease

stomach pain
crushing thirst
just enough to sleep

sneak slide down
hall slip back
between sheets

like whispers

tell no one
careful to leave
not even a crumb

one time

got caught
this girl said she'd snitch
if she couldn't come with us

take nothing back
we warned
but she didn't listen

left a trail of crumbs
from kitchen to bed
like arrows

could hear them
follow
down hall

click click click
of heels
on floor

swish swisssh
of black robes hunched
over in darkness

weetigo's hungry
for the carrion of children

runaway

even the fastest boy
the best swimmer

all sinew muscle and strong bone
got tracked dragged back

was almost home
he said

that priest
made him stand

arms outstretched
bible in each hand

in front of the school

so we could all witness
someone being saved

the sun blazed angry
turned the sky to fire

orange red pink
until embers

burned stars against
blue purple sky

still he stood
a Cree boy christ

until the world
finally burned

[sin]ew and bone
broken

knees buckled
bent over

at the feet
of the priest

a sacrifice
for our savage souls

oh yes
they were like otters

quick slipping
ripples

across our
skin

sliding
into our minds

they always found us
always

windows

kids stare
out windows

wait
any minute mama

papa will come
take me outta this place

scan bushes
look sharp

down
long winding road

a question
mark that ends

at residential school
the ultimate solution

to the indian
problem

in church
saints

look down
on us

sleepy eyes
languid lips

crimson mouths
mock

angels whisper
lie about miracles

stars shine
through dorm windows

cast shadows
across bodies

darker shadows rise
fall across our torsos

they prey in the dark
we pray silently

stare
out window

wait

for it to be over

the silent

creeps up
slow

shadow
of myself

crawls across
floor wall ceiling

anywhere but down there

makes sign of the cross
before slipping
away

out window
into black

blinks tear
shaped stars

full moon a drum
that never plays

shhh still
loud in my ear

the silent
is all i can tell you

the silent is still
here

loud in my ear
hissing

my heart beating
so fast

even still

in confession

those priests and nuns
they do bad things

with each other
and the girls too

even boys
dirty things

why God lets them do those things
i dunno

as for me
no one takes me like that

i fight back
kick that principal right in his balls

one time scratch that nun's face
they put me in the closet that time

but that's ok
i never get pregnant

get sent home like that
or worse

i always fight back
none of those girls

from back home
stick up for me

just harriet
and marie-rose

they are from pukatawagon
but that's ok

we stick together eh
they are my best friends

when i locked in that closet
they sneak bread under door

soak some water in so i don't die
crazy this place eh

in confession
after they let me out

i ask God
whose sins i confess

mine
or theirs

he never answered

calling down the sky

call us pagans
say we practice

devil worship
but those catholics

aren't from here
don't know nothing

about our night sky
her northern lights

never seen her
sky dance

us kids eh
conspire in Cree
pass notes

sneak past
praying nuns
in chapel
tonight

hide in tree line between
school and [am]bush

that night
green mist hung thick

shimmering shawl fringe
against black

that priest came out first
nuns behind him like ants

one lone whistle
slow and long

sliced through dark
a sound arrow

shrill trills
goose ducks loons
even moose calls
follow

sound snags shawl
we sing her to earth

ask her to dance
them into the sky

never seen
that priest run so fast

as though the devil
himself was chasing

nuns drop to their knees
scatter prayers like holy water

thrust crucifix
in every direction

before retreating
to their God building

not even he
could stop us

at least that night
us kids eh

we called down the sky
to save us

nīhithawan

by the time i am nine
the nuns have made me

a perfect parrot
spew bible verses

in latin french
and of course

in english
Cree a long lost echo

go back home for summer
look blank at everyone

chatter like a small swallow
in a sky full of ravens

it's great grannie annie
who takes me aside

whispers
nīhithawan

every day
for months

nīhithawan
breathes into my ear

retells every word
recreates every sound

nīhithawan
until i am again breathing

in my own voice
loud in my body

rosary

the nuns make me kneel
on pencil rows

hail mary
full of grace

over and over
hours and hours

until knees
bruise-beg

for mercy

but the blessed virgin mary
doesn't know

this moon-faced girl
from up north

doesn't speak
my language

she has no grace to spare

when i speak Cree
they beat me

word for word
until i have no words

just this prayer

hail mary
full of grace

in latin
in french

but never in Cree

until i don't pray
for mercy

just the will to survive
my arthritic knees

a testament
of my stubborn will

that not even
the mother of God

would scrape the Cree
from my bones

the last supper

sun rises a slow bear
summer hangs heavy

on the last day
of school i am 14

eager to escape
tight grip of nuns

who watch for last chance
to catch us being indian

late afternoon us girls
marie-rose harriet and me

sneak off into bush
pick berries

stick feet in cold lake
talk about what we'll do all summer

sly sun sneaks away too fast
soon it's dusk we lose our way back

track sneak into dining hall
slide into line like unseen foxes

oh but how we forget
these old crows catch everything

it's too late before i see her
feel grip quick violent

my head jerks back and forth
just as suddenly is free

look down at freshly cut braid
laying across my plate

my last supper

sister rose
holding scissors

her sharp smirk cuts
across my face

feel the blood rise
hot and mean

time stops

as if God is giving me
one last chance

to change my mind
but it's too late

i stand turn meet her
ash grey eyes wide in disbelief

grab her white yoke
twist back around flip her over

shoulder onto long table
kids dishes food

fly off in every direction
food specks across shocked faces

sister rose splayed out
in front of me

ball up my fists
hit her

again
and again

one for every hail mary
one for every bruise

one for each time
i had to kneel

one for each
of my broken bones

one for the first time
and the last time
she cut my hair

the sound of her shriek
of children chanting

the sound of my name

echoing loud
off walls

hidden traps

after residential school

i am sent to live
with my mother's mother

civilized and hand delivered
to her door

a stranger
in my own skin

a stranger to her
own kin

she does not love me
no one does

two five-gallon buckets of water
piles of wood on my back

every day
grandmother mary jane

no kindness in her bones
makes me work

harder than any nun or priest
marks food measures it

makes sure i don't eat any
hungry

and so tired
i run deep into bush

find the biggest tallest tree
strongest branches

climb that tree
find a long branch
thick with pine

line my thin body
along strong bough

sleep and dream
i am a bird

flying away

trapland

i want to give up

but these two little birds
one blue
one white
land just over dere

come on
astum
astum

they fly dis way
come back

mama tells me about the time
mary jane tries to lose her
in the trapland

go on ahead grandma says
watch for traps

late spring
caribou migration
moon a bright coin
against cobalt cold sky
mama walks west

wait uncle paul yells at me
points with whole arm
go dat way and don't durn

paul who always made sure
she didn't wander off

why you have to tell her
coulda lost that retard
for good

mama is used to that talk
from nuns at school

they don't believe her
when she tells them

she cannot hear
the word of God

call her slow stupid
retarded

sometimes she's grateful
the taunts are blurred

but grandmother's voice
crisp against early morning

rips into her ears
she turns away

leaves tear drop
tracks in snow

walks 80 miles straight
out of bush

the trapline fails to catch her
just like residential schools

she survives

everyone wants to know
how a half-deaf girl
makes it out alive

it was dose two little birds eh

mama pauses
cocks her head to one side
listening

dey sang me free

what is passed

mama confesses
i married a white man

to get away from this place
to escape the drinking

the silent violence
that rips us from each other

looks out window
but it never gets better

didn't know he would do the same
to my kids as those schools

didn't know i was running
from one hell into another

forty years i was with him
forty years my children

ripped up and run away from me
even as i watched hopeless

unable to scream enough
fight hard enough

i taught them nothing
except be tougher than the world

the burden of my failures
heavy on their shoulders

the faceless woman

mama dreams
about the party

everyone is there
drinking everywhere

people from back home
from school those long dead

twisted faces hollow eyes
hands clutch never empty bottles

mama says i sat in the corner
wondered where the door was

a woman sits next to me
turns her face

empty eye sockets
scrapped away nose

ears grown over
only her mouth

a gaping smear of red
my soundless scream

cannot wake me
the faceless woman

tells me
grow your hair long

it's the only way
to get rid of that nun

to finally escape this place
to find the exit

go back to the beginning
mama wakes

jukebox

mama at the door
purse in hand

friday to sunday
bar shoes on

i know she can already
hear the music

twang of second third fourth
beer buzzing her mind away

the open door is a jukebox
where the same song plays

over and over

mama looks past
my wet tears my only plea

before the song carries
her out

guy hill: august 4, 2012

mama stands at the foot
of the longest road

she ever travelled
ten hours northeast

down highway six
and fifty years back in time

mama returns
to where it began

a handwritten sign
reads guy hill

residential school gathering
an arrow points

down this dusty road
that marks so many

of her miles
ends all her questions

mama comes back
to take back

what was lost
along the shores

of clearwater lake
her little girl

waits

guy hill: the returning of souls

it seems smaller somehow
mama says looks over the grounds

rests hands on cane
peers over glasses

over there in that grove
that's where the blessed virgin mary sat

there was a fence over there
lip points left

boys and girls were separated eh
in those days going with someone

meant you waved at each other sometimes snuck
smokes and Cree words through fence

mama moves her eyes slow sifts through
each memory fitting it where it used to be

on land reclaimed by earth sky water
and survivors who come to find lost souls

over there is where the babies are buried
mama whispers at trees which whisper back

shhhhh but she is done being silent
those ones who didn't make it

those ones devoured by starvation
those sick ones who never got better

those who were taken
into rooms and never came out

i've seen them
those angels and demons

still out there
forever lost boys and girls

trying to find home
never got there

memorials

1.

guy hill residential school
long ripped down

a memorial marks
one of the dead here

a simple plaque
atop a concrete pillar

stands alone
on a small hill

for helen betty osborne
it reads

2.

survivors
turn it into a shrine

for all
who make
the pilgrimage

coins
rocks
jewellery

notes
pictures

open bibles
medicine bundles
a small glass pony

even a pink lace bra

left behind
to remember
or forget

3.

mama
takes my arm

slowly climbs
her way up a hill

that has taken
her fifty years

on the last day
of her return

we stand
together

lean in close
to worn faces

light fingertips
on fragile jewellery

gentle palm on pages
of scripture

read each piece
of story

inside the circle

4.

mama leaves
a broken piece

of brick she dug out
from dirt

from the school
she says

stares
for a long time

silent
they can have it back

turns toward home
early morning

breaks open
a new day

things i know about my mother as an adult

mama likes red rose tea
boiled in a pot
two tea bags

her tv programs
are soaps police shows
the young and the restless
csi hawaii 5-0

always cheers
when they catch the bad guy
gasps when her favourite
diva rises from the dead

mama yells in Cree at game shows
and every time stephen harper
is on the news

watches cooking shows
but never makes
carefully constructed dishes
says i just like how
pretty the food looks

every day
carefully measures
her blood adds subtracts
sugar injects insulin

counts the click click
of a disease taking away
her body

mama uses too much
toilet paper empty rolls
everywhere

keeps wads in pockets
they find way into laundry
bits of it all over sweaters

she is always too cold
too hot achy all over
or just too damn tired
all the time

has a pack of pills
to take care of all that
arrives weekly

in carefully constructed
bubbles labelled neatly
monday to sunday
repeat

she cannot sleep
in the dark alone
hangs string of lights
leaves hallway light on

wakes up over and over
to use bathroom
walks hallway
to escape nightmare
tries not to wake anyone

when mama is sick
i help her bathe
tuck her into flannel
piles of blankets heating pad

brush and brush her long hair
she's been growing
back four years now

grey roots flash
like a slip peaking out
from long black skirt

her thin strands
through my fingers
fragile threads
that connect us

i stay close watch
until her eyes close

mama finds sleep

i stay until her breath softens
rises
into dreams

when i think of mama in residential school

i think of my girls

my sun
first to reach my horizon

my moon
a dream come true

long lithe limbs
sweet berry mouths

brown eyes shimmer
skin burnished copper

if the indian agent came
commanded give me your children

if the mounties came
demanded stand aside

if the government came
declared it is the law

if they came for them
what would i do

would i call down the sun
would i call down the moon

if they came for my girls
would i call down the sky

what solace would i find
there in the silence

a gift of memories

as a baby
patch of dark hair
sharp brown eyes
chubby round cheeks
reflected sun
in her daddy's eyes

cradled in her mother's arms
genevieve glowing
her long dark hair loose
around them

barely one
and already running
oh she could run
if her daddy didn't catch her
she would run and run and run
her laughter stretched wide along horizons

her and kokum
flowered dress
kerchiefed head
braiding her granddaughter's
dark hair just so
ties it with moose hide strips

as a teenager
hip thrust out
cigarette held between
slender girl fingers
cat eye glasses
pointed and jewelled
she is smiling wide

a long thin Cree man
dangling around her neck
like a musical note
dark brown skin
wavy black hair
and oh the way he looks at her
like a country love song

a feast with all her favourites
moose meat fried onions
gravy potatoes even kfc
happy faces full stomachs

mama sitting in the middle
surrounded by her children
her long braids
her blue dress

these are pictures
of my mother

that do not exist

i would make them for her
a gift of memories

a box full for her to keep sacred
taken out at christmas time
or during long sunny afternoon

we would drink tea
look at each one
again and again

naming ceremony

a feast
moose hunted
in the fall time
berries picked
at their sweetest
rice potato pies
prepared all day

for a naming

offer tobacco
burn sage
sweetgrass
smoke rising
prayers inviting
ancestors
to ceremony

mama's name

i would name her
tallest pine tree woman

i would name her
take back woman

i would name her
makes her own blanket woman

i would name her
she makes a new path woman

i would name her
storm that breaks through woman

i would name her
north wind woman

i would call out
my mama's name

four times in each direction
so they never again forget

this naming ceremony
is my poem